CHICKENS
ARE LANDBOUND
A Journey to Identity and Sonship

FOREWORD BY
JONNATHAN ZIN TRUONG

CHICKENS
ARE LANDBOUND
A Journey to Identity and Sonship

RAYMOND YACKELL

Unless otherwise indicated, all scripture quotations are taken from the New King James Version of the Bible.

Scripture quotations taken from the Amplified® Bible (AMPC), © 1954, 1958, 1962, 1964, 1965, 1987 by The Lockman Foundation. Used by permission.

Scripture taken from The Message, © 1993, 1994, 1995, 1996, 2000, 2001, 2002 by NavPress Publishing Group. Used by permission.

Quotations from the book *Spiritual Slavery to Spiritual Sonship* by Jack Frost, © 2006 - Jack Frost, reproduced by permission of Destiny Image Publishers, Inc.

Flowing Rivers Ministries
9203 Hwy 6 South, Ste. 124, Box 192
Houston, Texas 77083
www.flowingrivers4u.org
flowingrivers@gmail.com

Copyright © 2017 by Raymond Yackell. All rights reserved.

Printed in the United States of America.

Reproduction of text in whole or in part without the express written consent by the author is not permitted and is unlawful according to the 1976 United States Copyright Act.

GOD MANIFEST PUBLISHING
www.godmanifestpublishing.com

This book and all other God Manifest Publishing and God Manifest Publishing Fiction books are available on Amazon.com.

Cover and Interior designed by Jonnathan Zin Truong
For more information on foreign distributors, email
publishers@godmanifestpublishing.com
Reach us at on the internet: www.godmanifestpublishing.com

ISBN: 978-1-7340556-5-8
eBook: ISBN: 978-1-7340556-6-5

TABLE OF CONTENTS

Acknowledgment 7

Foreword 9

Reflection 11

Introduction Why the Title 13

Testimony 15

Chickens & Eagles 19

Walls 25

Beware of the "Shoulds" 29

A Word About Ophans 33

Identity - Part 1 39

Identity - Part 2 43

Identity - True or False? 51

How Big Is Your "But"? 55

Trusting God 59

Intimacy & Sonship 65

Conclusion 71

Appendix A 75

ACKNOWLEDGMENT

I would like to thank Father God for saving me, loving me and changing me, Jesus for His sacrifice for me and His constant presence within me, and the Holy Spirit for guiding me, speaking to me, and inspiring me to write this book.

I would like to thank my wife, Sue, for putting up with me while I wrote this book. Her support and encouragement throughout the process has been awesome. I love you more than I can express.

I would like to thank my pastor, Grant Gomez, who spoke the Word of the Lord to me and encouraged me to write the book. Thank you for speaking the truth to me.

I would also like to thank Jonnathan and Olivia Truong, God Manifest Publishing, for their love, time, and lastly, their willingness to proofread, edit, and design this book. Love you guys.

Finally, I would like to thank my son, Ben, for our conversations about King David. Thanks for the different perspective.

FOREWORD

As a personal friend of Raymond Yackell and his wife Sue, I have seen God move mightily in their lives. As believers, the Yackells are as consistent as they come, seeking, hearing, and following God's voice through the toughest of times and the best of times. No matter the circumstance, my wife and I have watched in awe at their obedience to God's written and spoken Word. When I think about these two, one word comes to mind to describe them... radical.

These two are truly radical followers of Jesus Christ. Their fearless pursuit of freedom and liberty in the lives of those they encounter has freed many and released encounter to all.

Chickens Are Landbound is a must read for every Christian from all walks of life, whether you're freshly saved or a well season believer, this book on sonship will change your perspective on who God is in you and who you are in Him. The revelations within this book will surely realign your heart and mind to your position of sonship, within God's Kingdom and the endless possibilities for all who believe.

Be warned, once you pick up *Chickens Are Landbound*, you will not be able to put it down.

> **Isaiah 40:31 (NKJV)**
> But those who wait on the Lord
> Shall renew their strength;
> They shall mount up with wings like eagles,
> They shall run and not be weary,
> They shall walk and not faint.

Jonnathan Zin Truong
Author, *Buddhists, Mormons & Jesus*
Pastor, God Manifest - Houston, Texas

REFLECTION

One night, as I was lying quietly on my back before the Lord, I had a vision of a young man standing in front of what appeared to be a mirror. As he stood there, he was asking, "Who is that person in the mirror?" as though he didn't recognize his own reflection. I heard the Lord say to me, "There are many in My church, both young and old, who do not recognize themselves when they look in the mirror. The reason is because I am showing them a reflection of who I have created them to be, a reflection of how I see them. They have no idea who they are, and thus continue to search and search for that person in the mirror, not realizing that it is actually themselves, and all they have to do is turn to Me. For some, the person in the mirror scares them, because it isn't who they want to be, even though it is the person I have created them to be."

I have written this book at the direction of the Holy Spirit, with the purpose of bringing people to the mirror and showing them that the reflection in the mirror is who Father God created them to be. Throughout this book, I make reference to being a son of God. That does not preclude women from reading this book. I use the term "son" rather than "son/daughter" simply because it is easier to do and allowed the narrative to flow. I pray that this book will be a blessing to all who read it, regardless of gender.

INTRODUCTION
WHY THE TITLE?

I was in a meeting at Touched By Grace Ministries, I was quietly lying on my back before the Lord, focused on the Holy Spirit and soaking in His Presence, listening intently for the voice of God. I had been lying there for about 45 minutes under the heavy, weighty presence of the Lord. The only way I can describe that Presence, is that I felt like I was lying on the floor under several of those lead aprons that the dentist puts on you when they take x-rays. Such a heavy presence of the Lord, so peaceful and comforting, enveloped my entire being. After a while, I heard my name being called to come up and share what the Lord had put on my heart. It took several minutes for me to realize that my name was being called and that I was being summoned. When I finally reached the front of the sanctuary and took the microphone, I really had nothing to share until I heard the Lord speak into my thoughts and tell me to say "Chickens are landbound". At the time, it seemed such an odd thing to say. And the Lord said nothing else to me that evening. Several days later, when I was asking God about it, He told me that as children of God, we are to soar in the Spirit, and our place was soaring above and not pecking in the dirt.

This encounter ignited my journey to seek my identity in Him. I knew the Word of God said I was a child of God, but knowing wasn't enough. I needed to experience that I was His child, His son.

If you are in a place where you feel like you have hit a wall with your walk with God, a place where you are doing what you think the Lord wants, praying, fasting, attending church, being obedient, yet you feel like there is something missing, then read on. I was in the same place as you are, spiritually dissatisfied, hungering for more.

TESTIMONY

I met the Lord Jesus on January 1, 1983. My walk with the Lord since then has been one of growth and change. My wife and I served in several churches and under several pastors. We were faithful to attend church and to be in the Word. Yet I still didn't have the relationship with God that I heard others had, nor did I really know how to go about getting that relationship. I continued to serve God, doing everything I could to make sure I got His approval, working out my salvation through works as discussed in Philippians 2:12. My born-again life had stagnated at the foot of the cross, never moving into the resurrection life. I saw the Lord begin to use my wife in her prophetic gift, and I felt as though I was being left behind. So again, I made sure that I was "doing stuff for the Lord" so that I would get His approval, as well as man's. I was a people pleaser because of my insecurities and what I thought was the necessity to please God by my works.

In 1997, things changed because we began a new, deeper walk with God that many refer to as "the River". My life was changed, and I started to believe that I no longer had to work to be accepted by God. I realized acceptance had been accomplished on the cross by Jesus. I continued in my walk with God, seeing more and more manifestations of His love for me and a transformation in my spirit, but it still wasn't enough. There still seemed to be something missing. I continued to serve God with everything I had and didn't feel like I had to work for His approval, yet I knew there was more. I knew there was a deeper level of intimacy with God that was still beyond my grasp. Then one day, as I was attending a Father's Heart conference in Houston, it became clear to me that I was living my spiritual life as an orphan, rather than a son.

That realization and the transformation from "spiritual orphan" to "spiritual son" changed my life forever. It provided me with my true identity in Him, an identity that no one can take away from me: the identity of being a child of God who fully experiences the Father's love for me as a son. As a child of God, I no longer care about pleasing people, only pleasing my Father God. I love people, but I don't have to please them. I no longer have to have their approval and acceptance to validate myself. My Father in heaven validates me. I am loved. The death of Jesus on the cross means that I am of value to the Father. No one and nothing can convince me otherwise, because I don't just acknowledge the love of the Father intellectually, I have experienced the love of the Father.

The difference between knowing something intellectually and experiencing it is dramatic. The intellectual knowledge of a thing can be challenged and refuted, and the next wind of doctrine or the next message can change what you know. Your experience of something cannot be refuted. As Acts 4:20 says, "We cannot stop speaking of what we have seen and heard." People can say that what you experienced isn't real, but you know what you experienced. No one can take away your experiences, only you can decide to deny them.

Romans 8:19-22 says, "For the earnest expectation of the creation eagerly waits for the revealing of the sons of God. For the creation was subjected to futility, not willingly, but because of Him who subjected it in hope, because the creation itself also will be delivered from the bondage of corruption into the glorious liberty of the children of God. For we know that the whole creation groans and labors with the birth pangs together until now."

This passage of scripture tells us that even creation is waiting for the sons of God to be revealed, for us to take our rightful place. Creation was corrupted when Adam and Eve fell, and it has been waiting for the time when the sons of God would stand up and set things right, even in creation, when we would again take dominion. The sons of God can reverse the curse for us. When we stand in the position of sons, knowing the will of God and our authority as sons of God, we can command creation, just as Jesus did with the wind and the waves. If the sons of God would stand in agreement and pray, we could heal the ozone layer, we could reverse so-called global warming, we could heal creation from its corruption at the hands of the enemy. If we, as sons of God, would band together as a body, as the Father envisions us to be, we could pray and declare this planet provide for us until such time as the Lord returns. That is the power available to the sons of God and the body of Christ according to Romans 8:19-22.

CHICKENS & EAGLES

Fear is a powerful force in the world today. Fear will keep us from doing the will of God. Fear will prevent us from yielding to and accepting our identity in Him. The thing is we have a powerful force of our own, and that is the Spirit of God.

2 Timothy 1:7 says, "For God has not given us a spirit of fear, but of power and of love and of a sound mind."

Think about that for a minute. We have been given a spirit of power, the Greek word here is "dunamis," which means "power, force or ability." When the woman touched Jesus' garment as told in Mark 5:30, He felt "dunamis" go out of him, so this power is miracle-working power.

We have been given a spirit of love, not just any kind of love, but agape love, unconditional love, the God kind of love.

And a sound mind, the Greek word used here, "sophronismos," means discipline or self-control.

So, we have been given miracle-working power, God's unconditional love, and discipline. These are attributes of our identity. What can we accomplish with these tools in our spiritual tool belt?

The Lord illustrated this to me through a comparison between chickens and eagles.

Chickens

1. Run for cover in a storm.
2. Protect their chicks and teach them how to find food.
3. Will mate with any chicken.
4. See only their immediate surroundings.
5. When chickens start to molt, other chickens will peck the one molting, sometimes to the death.

Eagles

1. Spread their wings and soar into and/or above the storm, thus getting through it quicker.

2. Raise their young to independence. Eaglets leave the nest on their own at about 10-12 weeks old. The adult eagles will sometimes put food nearby for the fledgling eaglet to try his wings and feed itself. Once strong enough to fly, juvenile eagles will stay in the nesting territory for 4-12 weeks, learning to hunt and fly from their parents before going off on their own.

3. Select a mate based on certain criteria, and then mate for life. Below is an example of the criteria used,

4. Have tremendous eyesight and far-reaching vision.

5. Both eagle parents participate in the rearing of eaglets.

6. Eagles don't eat dead things.

Researchers have observed male and female eagles going through a mating ritual, where the female will grab a stick and fly up high, then drop the stick to see if the male can catch it before it hits the ground. The female will repeat this ritual several times, flying higher each time before dropping the stick. If the male chases after and catches the stick each time before it hits the ground, the female will mate with him. The reason for this little mating game is to determine the commitment of the male. It's a bit of a test conducted by the female before she trusts the male. Men, can you imagine if a variation of this criterion was used to determine your suitability as husband material?

Eagles fly into the face of the storm and get through it more quickly. Many other birds hunker down and wait out the storm, like the chicken who runs for cover. However, the eagle flies into the face of the storm or above it without thought, without reasoning, just on instinct, because the eagle knows who he is and who his creator made him to be.

We all have storms in our lives. We can react like chickens and tuck our heads and run for cover, hoping that the whole situation will pass, or we can act like the eagles we were created to be and stand in the face of the storm or soar right through the storm with the Spirit of God.

Storms sometimes keep us from the promises of God. Many times, we are on the verge of a breakthrough into God's promise, but we decide that the storm is too much, and we quit.

We should face the storm with the Lord rather than try and run away from it or reason it out, wondering, "Why is this happening to me?" For example, early in our walk with God, my wife and I struggled financially. We didn't complain, we didn't give up, we continued to pay our tithe and give offerings whenever the Lord told us to. We simply relied upon the Word of God in Malachi 3:10-11, which tells us to bring all the tithe to the storehouse, and when we do, the windows of heaven will be opened for us and a blessing will be poured out upon us that we won't have room to receive. We relied on Luke 6:38 that says, "Give and it will be given to you, pressed down, shaken together and running over." We did those very things, even though those in the world today would have told us we were crazy. As a result of turning into the financial storm and continuing to give, we came through that financial struggle blessed in our finances to the point that we could be a blessing to others who struggle in their finances. We could have gotten into a bunker mentality and stopped giving until things were better financially, but that is not what the Word of God says to do. We chose to soar in the spirit like the eagle, rather than be like a chicken.

We should go through the storm and watch what the Lord works through as our faith is proven and strengthened. As believers, we face spiritual storms, and we never go through the storm alone. The Holy

Spirit is with us throughout. We should face the storm in the Spirit as naturally as the eagle does in the natural. When we do, then we come to a place where we know who we are in Him and who He is in us.

WALLS

Exodus 20:5 says, "You shall not bow down to them nor serve them (speaking of other gods). For I, the Lord your God, am a jealous God, visiting the iniquity of the fathers upon the children to the third and fourth generations of those who hate Me. *(parentheses added)*"

This verse speaks specifically about idolatry, but iniquity (defined as wickedness or sin in the dictionary, and the word in Hebrew is "avown," which means perversity or sin) is also included in the generational curses or sins of the fathers that are passed down from generation to generation. Some of these iniquities are the family secrets that no one really talks about, but everyone seems to know (I've often wondered, if nobody talks about them, how come everyone knows about them?). Because of the shame associated with these secrets, we build walls that help protect us from the shame, forcing us to protect ourselves so that people won't find out. "What if so-and-so found out I was _____ (you fill in the blank), they would judge me or reject me." So, we keep it a secret, even from God (or so we think).

As we live our lives, things happen to cause us to sin, or things happen that cause hurts, wounds, and offenses to come. In many cases, these hurts and offenses, and our sin cause us to add to our walls, because we don't want to be hurt again. We don't want to be wounded again; we don't want others to know we have these shortcomings and sin in our lives. So we add another brick in the wall around our heart so that nothing and no one can get in, and eventually we have even walled ourselves off from God. The devil would try to convince us that because of our sin, shame, or generational issues, that God cannot or will not love us anymore.

Those walls that we put up to protect ourselves, actually prevent us from walking in our true identity, and for some of us, we have been walled off for so long that when we look in the mirror, we don't recognize our true selves anymore. We spend so much time trying to hide who we really are, that we have forgotten who we really are. This condition is called an identity crisis, defined by Webster's as "the condition of being uncertain about one's self, especially with regard to character, goals, origins". Our faith and trust begin to be in those walls of protection rather than in God. Those walls prevent us from being the relational people that we are created to be. The walls prevent us from having a true and intimate relationship with others as well as God. We hide, we wear masks, we don't allow people to know who we really are, and our relationships are all superficial, if we can sustain relationships at all.

We were created to be relational people. We were created to interact with one another and with God. The walls we have set up are not conducive to having true, intimate relationships because we are incapable of allowing people to know who we really are, providing we know ourselves. Walls hide our true identities, so that we feel safe. No one sees the real you, so you don't have to worry about people finding out about _____. And in so doing, you have actually lost your true self. Without being yourself, you cannot have a truly intimate relationship with anyone, including God.

Before we became believers, the walls served the purpose of protecting us. Unfortunately, this means that we don't trust as we should, which then flows over to our relationship with God, and hinders our faith and trust in Him. After we become believers, we no longer need to defend ourselves, we no longer need the walls, because God is our protector.

Will you have the trust and faith to believe that? Read Psalms 91 for encouragement to trust and have faith in God our protector.

Ephesians 4:21-24 says, "If indeed you have heard Him and have been taught by Him, as the truth is in Jesus, that you put off, concerning your former conduct, the old man which grows corrupt according to the deceitful lusts, and be renewed in the spirit of your mind, and that you put on the new man, which was created according to God, in true righteousness and holiness."

Behind the walls, we don't think we're righteous or holy because of sin, wound or offense, but verse 24 says that the new man was created according to God in true righteousness and holiness. God loves us so much that He accepts us just the way we are, and He also loves us too much to leave us that way. The walls of unforgiveness, bitterness, hurt, and offense keep us in bondage, causing us to attempt to control our environment and those who happen to cross our path. That desire for control prevents us from having a real relationship with anyone, unless it is on our terms, including our relationship with God. Our mindset is something like, "As long as God responds to me on my terms, then we are good." When this doesn't happen, we get angry at God. That sort of one-sided relationship is unhealthy, unrealistic, and unsustainable.

BEWARE OF THE "SHOULDS"

In 1 Samuel 17, King Saul tries to give David his armor to wear before going out to battle Goliath. David, in turn, says that he cannot wear it because he hadn't proven or tested the armor. It wasn't his armor to wear. Saul was trying to put David into his (Saul's) own mold, but David stood in his own identity instead. Had he acted in any other manner, he would have struggled against Goliath.

We must also stand against those who would attempt to put us in their mold, trying to make us fit into the identity they have for us, no matter how well-meaning their intentions may be. Our identity is unique in that we have been uniquely created and formed. The Bible says that we have been fearfully and wonderfully made (Psalms 139:14). We have been given the nature of God, and it is manifesting in each of our lives in a unique way, if we will only allow it, and stop trying to be like everyone else or please everyone. Our experiences cause us to react in different ways, God uses those reactions for His purposes as well. Nothing goes to waste with God. Our reactions to various situations are part of our uniqueness. Others will try to put you into a box of their own design, for a variety of reasons, not all of them godly reasons. If someone says, "You should be this way or that way," this is a red flag warning to be wary, because not all of the "you shoulds" are helpful. Many may pull us out of our identity and push us into the identity that others see for us.

Your identity is the key to your destiny. If you step out of your identity, then you step out of your destiny. And you must know your identity in Him before you can ever step into His destiny for you

Those believers who fall when temptation comes, do so because they have either forgotten their identity, dismissed it, or have intentionally walked away from it. When you know your identity in God and walk in it, temptation loses its power, because sin is not a natural state in your Godly identity. For example, in 2 Samuel 11, David is supposed to be off to battle, but instead he goes up on the rooftop and sees Bathsheba bathing. Temptation comes, David succumbs to it, and commits adultery by force, and, later, murder to cover up his adultery, all because he stepped out of his identity as the king. He decided he wasn't going to do what kings do at that particular time of year.

2 Samuel 11:1-2 "It happened in the spring of the year, <u>at the time when kings go out to battle</u>, that David sent Joab and his servants with him, and all Israel; and they destroyed the people of Ammon and besieged Rabbah. But David remained at Jerusalem.

Then it happened one evening that David arose from his bed and walked on the roof of the king's house. And from the roof he saw a woman bathing, and the woman was very beautiful to behold."

Verse 1 specifically says "...at the time when kings go out to battle". It doesn't say when kings send their armies out to battle, but when kings go out to battle. David was supposed to be leading his armies against Ammon and besieging Rabbah. By not being where he was supposed to be and doing what he was supposed to be doing in accordance with his identity as the king, he was tempted and succumbed to that temptation. We must not only guard our hearts, but we must guard our identity, for the enemy will try to cause us to relinquish it.

God is our Father, not our boss, not a harsh taskmaster, therefore we are in the position of sons, children of God. We are His children, not His hirelings, not His servants. Even though we serve Him, it is not from the position of a slave or servant, but out of love for Him as His son or daughter.

The heart of our identity is that we are the House of God, His dwelling place. 1 Corinthians 3:16 (AMP) says that we are the temple of God and that God's Spirit has His permanent dwelling within us. 1 Peter 2:5 says, "[Y]ou also, as living stones, are built up a spiritual house..."

We are the House of God on this earth, and as the House of God on the earth, we are to bring heaven to earth.

Matthew 6:10 says, "Your Kingdom come, Your will be done, on earth as it is in heaven."

God's not going to bring heaven to earth, He is expecting us, as His sons and daughters, to do it. Throughout the Bible, you can see examples of God doing things on the earth, but He has usually used a person to do it.

The ability and authority to partner with God for His will to be done on earth requires us to have a relationship with God, not just religion. Religion is form without power. Religion points to man's rites and traditions, things should be done in this manner and according to this format. Having a relationship with the Father means that He is revealing Himself and His will to us. He reveals the things of God to us through His Holy Spirit, according to 1 Corinthians 2:9-10.

Doesn't Matthew 6:10 say "Your kingdom come, Your will be done on earth as it is in heaven"? How can we do the will of God if we don't know what His will is? We can know His will by spending time developing a relationship with the Father, a relationship that will take time to nurture and develop. We can also know His will by reading His Word.

1 John 5:14-15 says "Now this is the confidence that we have in Him, that if we ask anything according to His will, He hears us. And if we know that He hears us, whatever we ask, we know that we have the petitions that we have asked of Him."

Religion won't get you to a position of knowing His will, but having an actual relationship with the Father most certainly will. Getting that relationship right with God will help you in your earthly relationships.

A WORD ABOUT ORPHANS

This book addresses the issue of identity and sonship. The alternative to sonship is an orphan spirit. An orphan is one who does not feel like they have any value in the heart of the Father, like they don't have a home. The Bible tells us in Romans, chapter 8, that we have been given the spirit of adoption, thereby no longer being an orphan.

Have you stepped out of that orphan spirit and into the position of a son? Many of us have a "command and obey" relationship with God. He commands and we obey. Command and obey, command and obey. Servants of God, I would say that He isn't looking for mere servants. He isn't looking for prophets. He isn't looking for apostles. He isn't looking for pastors. He is looking for sons who will stand in the positions needed to fulfill His plans and purposes here on the earth.

Prophecy, from an earthly perspective, is simply man speaking God's word. However, prophecy, from a heavenly perspective, is the Father speaking to His sons. Orphan-spirited Christianity is about doing what God tells you to do, as mentioned above, it is command and obey, no relationship with the Father or the Spirit of God. Do you want to be a prophet just to hear God speak, or do you want to be a son and have the Father speak to you? There is a difference. One has the mentality of a servant, and one has the mentality of a son.

Orphan-spirited Christians haven't experienced the love of the Father. They know that He loves them and that Jesus loves them (John 3:16 tells us that), but they haven't felt and experienced the Father's love for themselves.

Many of the following list of traits of both the orphan-spirited Christian and sons have been taken from the book *Spiritual Slavery to Spiritual Sonship* by Jack Frost (see Appendix A).

The orphan-spirited Christian exhibits some of the following traits:

1. Sees God as Master/Commander, someone to be obeyed
2. Independent and self-reliant
3. Live by the love of the law (rules, principles, religion, tradition)
4. Insecure, but cover it well (strive to act right, do enough to please God and people)
5. Servant-focused, waiting and listening for a command to obey
6. Looking for a reward or blessing for their obedience. What they want is a blessing from God or recognition from man.
7. Put God in a box, putting everyone in the mold of "You have to do things this way or according to this formula"
8. Their walk is a competition, a rivalry, and there is jealousy when others succeed
9. See authority as a source of pain, therefore they are usually suspicious of any authority except their own
10. Generally unteachable
11. Guarded and conditional in their expression of love. What can you do for me?

Sons, on the other hand, exhibit some of the following traits:

1. See God as a loving Father
2. Interdependent, rely on the Holy Spirit. They need the community of love that God and the body of Christ offer.
3. Live by the law of love (receiving love from the Father and giving it away)

4. Secure and at peace and rest in the Father's embrace

5. Obey out of their love for the Father, not for reward acceptance, or approval

6. Work with God and want to be a blessing to God

7. Let God be God, knowing His thoughts and His ways are higher than theirs

8. Relate to peers through humility and unity as they honor and value others, rejoicing in their blessing and success

9. Respectful, honoring legitimate authority

10. Teachable

11. Open, transparent, and affectionate in their expression of love. What can I do for you?

When you are asked what you want to do for God, what is your answer? Some would say "Oh, I just want to do His will". That's a good thing to want to do His will, but it can also be a cop-out. Do you have Kingdom dreams? What would you like to do with God? Take it to God and He may just say to you, "Yes, son, let's do that together." What would you do for God if you knew that you couldn't fail? What are you waiting for? Go and do it, because it was put on your heart for a reason.

Sonship is freedom. As a son, you can relate to God in your own way, no formula necessary. However, what worked for me might not work for you, so that's why this is not a how-to book. You have your own unique walk with the Lord. My assignment is not your assignment, and your assignment is not mine. Sonship releases us to use the creativity that God has put inside each and every one of us. We need to tap into it, and that process starts with being a son and not a servant.

As our sonship relationship grows, and we grow to love what God loves, we start to ask "Father, can I do this?," rather than "What do you want me to do?" Notice that sons ask permission rather than waiting around for a command. This dynamic reveals an entirely different relationship. Our time with the Father shouldn't only be about praying and listening, but it should also be about communing with Him, loving Him, thanking Him.

IDENTITY - PART 1

Many mighty men and women of God who have accomplished great feats have lost sight of who they are in God, in essence losing their identity. We see men and women of God throughout scripture who, for whatever reason, did not walk into the fullness of what God had for them immediately, or somehow faltered.

For example, in 1 Kings 17:1, we see the boldness of the prophet Elijah who went to King Ahab and announced that there would not be rain in the land except at his (Elijah's) word. In 1 Kings 18:19-40, Elijah calls out all Israel and the prophets of Baal, and says, "Whichever god answers with fire, let him be God." The prophets of Baal shout and pray and dance and cut themselves, but Baal doesn't answer. Elijah douses his altar with water (not once, but three times) and calls on God, who then answers with fire, consuming the sacrifice Elijah prepared as well as the water that they had poured on the altar. Then Elijah ordered the prophets of Baal seized and executed. Afterward, Queen Jezebel threatens Elijah, who gives into fear, losing sight of who he is in God. Notice in 1 Kings 19:3, it says "And when he saw that, he arose and ran for his life..." Elijah saw in his mind's eye what Jezebel had threatened. He focused on the words Jezebel spoke rather than focusing on the Lord. By doing so, he stepped out of his identity as the prophet of God.

We, in turn, have to keep the eyes of our spirit on Father God, otherwise the enemy and/or our flesh will cause us to step out of our identity in Him.

Another example of this is Peter, who at one point denied Jesus three times. Peter was told that God had revealed Jesus' identity to him, and then a scant few minutes later was told, "Get behind me, Satan" (Matthew 16:17 and 16:23, respectively). Peter was a man who was unsure of his identity. After the death and resurrection of Jesus, even after Jesus had appeared to others, Peter said to the other disciples, "I'm going fishing" (John 21:3). He had resigned himself to go back to what was familiar to him, fishing. Remember Jesus spoke to Peter and told him, "Upon this rock (Peter) I will build my church" (Matthew 16:18). Jesus actually speaks Peter's identity to him, but Peter doesn't receive it. In his mind, he is still a fisherman, rather than a fisher of men. His mind hasn't been transformed. He doesn't know who he is, and as a result, he is confused about his identity, so he goes back to what he knows, what he is comfortable with, fishing.

Jesus told Peter the following,

Matthew 16:19 "And I will give you the keys of the kingdom of heaven, and whatever you bind on earth will be bound (to deprive of liberty) in heaven and whatever you loose on earth will be loosed (set free, dissolved, severed) in heaven." *(parentheses added).*

We have been given the keys to the kingdom, we have been given the authority to bind and loose. Binding and loosing is just what it sounds like, only in the spirit realm. Binding is to tie something up, loosing is to free something up. For example, when attacked with depression, for no real reason, you can pray to bind that spirit of depression, command it to go, and then loose a spirit of joy.

Matthew 12:28-29 says "But if I cast out demons by the Spirit of God, surely the kingdom of God has come upon you. Or how can one enter a strong man's house and plunder his goods, unless he first binds the strong man?

Do you:

1. know that you have that authority, and
2. do you believe that you have that authority?

It's not just the Word of God in the scripture, but do you KNOW, beyond a shadow of a doubt that you have this authority to bind and loose? Sure, the Bible says so, but the Bible says a lot of things that people read, but don't believe apply to them. Some say, "Oh, that died out with the apostles." If that's the case, then why do people today get healed at the hands of ministers who pray for the sick? Why are there still miracles, signs, and wonders, if it all died with the apostles? Yes, Jesus was speaking to Peter, but anything in the scripture is accessible to every believer. Acts 10:34 says that God is no respecter of persons.

IDENTITY - PART 2

We all have an identity, even before we were born or born again as believers in Jesus.

Jeremiah 1:5 (AMP) "Before I formed you in the womb I knew you and approved of you as My chosen instrument, and before you were born I separated and set you apart, consecrating you; and I appointed you as a prophet to the nations."

Before we were even formed in the womb, God knew us. He knew His plan for us. He knew our ups and He knew our downs, and yet He still has a plan and a destiny for each and every one of us, both those who will serve Him and those who won't.

Some would say that this passage of scripture shows that our life here on earth is predetermined and there isn't anything that we can do about it. If that were so, then the free will that God gave us would be null and void. He gave us free will to decide. **God has predetermined your design, but He has not predetermined your desire.** How hungry are you for the things of God? Your desire and hunger for the things of God will determine the depth of your intimacy with the Father and your ability to hear from Him and walk into your God-given destiny.

Throughout the Bible, God's people are called servants, however, in John 15:14-15, Jesus calls His disciples friends. After His death and resurrection, Jesus called them brothers (John 20:17). If He called them brothers, that means that they were sons of God. If we are God's children, does that mean we cease to be servants? Of course not, it just means that we have the heart of a servant and the spirit of a son. The heart of a servant is that we desire to serve out of our love for the Father, not because we have to serve. Didn't Jesus tell the disciples that the greatest among them would be servant of all? Sonship is a position, not a title. Titles carry no power, though many would seek a title thinking that the authority comes with the title. Seek to be a son, because sons have the authority of the Father. In Romans chapter 8, the Bible tells us that if we are led by the Spirit of God, then we are the sons of God, if sons, then co-heirs with Jesus.

Romans 8:14-17 says, "For as many as are led by the Spirit of God, they are the sons of God

For you have not received the spirit of bondage again to fear, but you have received the Spirit of adoption, whereby we cry, Abba Father.

The Spirit itself bears witness with our spirit, that we are the children of God

And if children, then heirs; and joint heirs with Christ; if so be that we suffer with Him, that we may be glorified together."

Your true identity on this earth as a believer is that you are a son of God. This is not something that you try to become. You simply are. A pastor friend of mine once said that a favorite trick of the devil is to cause us to try and become what we already are. That was the case in my life before I understood that I was a son of God.

Let's look at Gideon in the sixth chapter of Judges. We see Gideon toiling away, hiding from the Midianites as he threshes wheat. The angel of the Lord appears to Gideon, and in verse 12, the angel greets Gideon as God sees him ("The Lord is with you, mighty man of valor.") In verse 14, the angel tells him to go and deliver Israel from the Midianites ("Go in this might of yours, and you shall save Israel from the hand of the Midianites. Have I not sent you?"). In verse 15, Gideon tells the angel how he sees himself ("O Lord, how can I save Israel? Indeed **my clan is the weakest** in Manasseh, and **I am the least** in my father's house."). Gideon eventually gives in to his destiny after setting out two fleeces to prove the Lord's assignment.

In another example, in Numbers chapter 13, the Lord tells Moses to send 12 spies to the land that the Lord has promised to give to Israel. The spies went, and returned bringing with them some of the fruit of the land. Then the spies gave their report.

Numbers 13:27-33 "Then they told him, and said: 'We went to the land where you sent us. It truly flows with milk and honey, and this is its fruit.

Nevertheless the people who dwell in the land are strong, the cities are fortified, and very large, moreover we saw the descendants of Anak there.

The Amalekites dwell in the land of the South, the Hittites, the Jebusites, and the Amorites dwell in the mountains, and the Canaanites dwell by the sea and along the banks of the Jordan.'

Then Caleb quieted the people before Moses, and said, 'Let us go up at once and take possession, for we are well able to overcome it.'

But the men who had gone up with him said, 'We are not able to go up against the people, for they are stronger than we.'

And they gave the children of Israel a bad report of the land which they had spied out, saying, 'The land through which we have gone as spies is a land that devours its inhabitants, and all the people whom we saw in it are men of great stature.

There we saw the giants (the descendants of Anak came from the giants) and <u>we were like grasshoppers in our own sight</u>, and so we were in their sight.'"

What an incredibly profound and damaging statement we see in Numbers 13:33. Note that it says **"we were like grasshoppers in our own sight."** They determined their identity, which was completely out of line with God's identity for them. This statement negated their ability to partake in the promise. They had admitted that the land was a land "flowing with milk and honey," just as God had promised. The Lord saw them as conquerors. The Lord already saw them as inhabitants of that land, the land of promise. The Israelites were having an identity crisis – they were continuing in their identity as slaves in Egypt, rather than inheritors of the Promised Land. Throughout their journey from

Egypt to the Promised Land, there are examples of this mindset. Many times they complained and accused Moses of bringing them out of Egypt to simply die in the desert. They didn't see Moses as their deliverer, but merely as someone who had talked them into leaving their luxurious lives (talk about selective memory) of slavery back in Egypt. The Israelites were comfortable back in Egypt, or at least as they misremembered it, they were comfortable. They had become accustomed to the day-to-day drudgery of slavery for the Egyptians. It was difficult work, but it was all they knew, and they had grown accustomed to that life.

Stepping out and traveling to the Promised Land to become what God had promised their father Abraham was outside their comfort zone. It required faith and trust in God: a faith and trust that He would do what He said He would do. They never gave Him a chance to prove it, because they did not obey and go into the Promised Land. The bad report of the spies convinced the nation of Israel that they would be defeated and killed if they attempted to go into the Promised Land. Will you forgo your Promised Land? Will you forgo your destiny in Him because you don't have the faith and trust in the promise or the One who gave you the promise?

As mentioned before, an identity crisis is defined as the condition of being uncertain about one's self, especially with regard to character, goals, and origins. Have you ever said, or thought, "I know what the Bible says and I believe it, but have a hard time believing that God will do it through me?" That is, by definition, a spiritual identity crisis. You are thinking like a spiritual orphan. In that place, you are like the Israelites, a grasshopper in your own sight.

There is a constant battle going on in the spiritual realm, a battle for our destiny, a battle that forces us to a place of decision. Which reality will we follow? The reality of the flesh and what we see, or the reality of the spirit that is orchestrated by God? The fleshly reality is limited to what we see and understand. The spiritual reality is not only unlimited, but one of love, joy, and perfection in Him. Are we perfect? Of course not, but God sees perfection in each of His children. God sees us as the finished product, not the work in progress.

Remember how the angel greeted Gideon? Unfortunately, we tend to look at ourselves with the natural eye and sometimes we don't like what we see. We aren't handsome enough, pretty enough, tall enough, rich enough, thin enough, strong enough, whatever shortcomings we see. We buy into the delusion forged by the devil that we are somehow damaged goods, and we find ourselves disliking and sometimes even hating this thing or that thing about ourselves. It's a delusion, people!!! A lie from the pit of hell!!!

Genesis 1:26 says, "Then God said, 'Let us make man in Our image (resemblance, representative figure), according to Our likeness (nature or personality); let them have dominion over the fish of the sea, over the birds of the air, and over the cattle, over all the earth and over every creeping thing that creeps on the earth.'" *(parenthetical comments added)*.

We have been created in the image of God and with the personality of God, yet we see ourselves in such a lowly way, diminishing that truth. Identity crisis means spiritual orphan. Any time that we see ourselves as something other than sons and daughters of God, we have stepped into the delusion of the enemy. We have forgotten who we are, and that we were made in God's image. When we surrender ourselves to God, and see ourselves as He sees us, we will walk in peace because we will come to the realization that this is the truth of who we are and what we are supposed to be, created in His image and with His nature. He loves, so because we have His nature, we love. For in 1 John 4:8 it says, "He who does not love does not know God, for God is love."

This is the place of truth. Reality is different than truth because you can alter your reality by simply perceiving things differently. The manner in which you think about a situation can change the reality of the situation, simply because different experiences will cause you to react differently to a situation. I'm not talking about facts – facts are facts. You can't change them, but your reaction to those facts can be different. Absolute truth (God's truth) is truth, not someone's perception of the truth, regardless of the situation or your experience.

Isaiah 64:8 says, "But now, O Lord, you are our Father; We are the clay, and You our potter; And all we are the work of Your hand."

So are you a good little lump of clay, willing to allow God to form you into whatever He wants you to be? Or do you keep jumping off the potter's wheel because you think you know what you are supposed to be? Are you like the clay in Isaiah 45:9 "...shall the clay say to him who forms it, 'What are you making?'" Are you that lump of clay? Are you mad at God because He didn't make YOUR plan work out?

God's anointing for you may be for the Helps ministry, where you help out doing whatever sort of thing that that the ministry needs to have done, from cleaning bathrooms to ushering. But you may think your anointing should be worship, so you try to make God work out your plan. When He doesn't, you get mad. God is the potter, and you are the clay, not the other way around.

We need to come into agreement with God, not try to get God to come into agreement with us. This causes identity crisis because it isn't working out for us the way WE planned. We get discouraged because OUR plan didn't work out, so we think God won't work through us. When we come to grips with our true identity in Him and begin to walk in it, then we access the power of being a child of God. We walk in our true reality and identity, our true destiny, and we are no longer in that state of delusion and identity crisis, because we have begun to see ourselves as God sees us. We are what God says we are.

The issue is, which will you choose, the delusion the devil and the world proposes, or the reality and identity that God has for you? Will you choose the reality that says that you are loved no matter what, you are accepted by the Father, you are His child? That is the reality that Father God has for you.

IDENTITY - TRUE OR FALSE?

These days, when you look on social media, much of what you see is selfie after selfie. Many people will take selfie after selfie to get just the right one to post. Your selfie is not who you are, it merely shows your earth suit, the container for your spirit.

Romans 4:17 says, "(as it is written, "I have made you a father of many nations") in the presence of Him whom he believed, who gives life to the dead and <u>calls those things which do not exist as though they did</u>."

Paul was talking about Abraham here (father of many nations), but at the time that God called Abraham the father of many nations, Abraham was not even a father to Isaac. God was calling him something that currently wasn't as though it were. That is because God always sees us as we were created to be. Remember in Judges chapter 6, the angel of the Lord greets Gideon by calling him a mighty man of valor. Gideon wasn't in his own eyes, but God saw him that way. God sees us the same way. He sees us as He created us to be, not as we are in our own eyes or the eyes of others.

Many today get their identity from what they do for a living, or their place in a family. Your identity is not in what you do for a living or whether you are a husband, wife, mom, or dad. As a believer, your identity is that you are a son of God. However, it is up to you to walk in this identity. You have to decide to run your race with Him. You have to decide to walk in the destiny that God has for you. YOU HAVE TO DECIDE. You have to know your identity in Him before you can ever step into the destiny that He has for you.

In 1 Samuel 17:31-37, David decides to go up against Goliath.

1 Samuel 17:37 "Moreover David said, 'The Lord, who delivered me from the paw of the lion and from the paw of the bear, He will deliver me from the hand of this Philistine.' And Saul said to David, 'Go and the Lord be with you!'"

David knew who he was in the Lord, and he knew what he could accomplish with the Lord. We all know the results of this story. David slew Goliath and then went on to fulfill the destiny God had for him.

What would you do for God if you knew that you couldn't fail or be defeated? Well go and do it, because it's on your heart because God put it there. We have to make sure that we stay in His will and do things according to His direction. Staying in that place of obedience to Him keeps us on the path to our purpose and destiny.

Some of what we think of as natural talent are really giftings from God. Those giftings are part of your godly identity. Some of the things that you will do for God will come so naturally and effortlessly that it won't seem like it's a big deal. But to others it will be like signs and wonders. Like, WOW!!!

Step into the place of self-denial, denying yourself the over-indulgence in your life in whatever form it takes. Let's deny who our worldly-inspired flesh thinks we are or others think we should be (especially if we are seeking their approval, because God's approval is all we need). You will never be able to get everyone's approval, because there will always be someone out there who will be upset about anything that you do. The enemy will always make sure that there will be someone who is disappointed, jealous, or simply in disagreement. When you step deeper into the things of God, some of your well-meaning friends will tell you that you may need to find balance in your life, and not to get too radical for God (as if there is such a thing). Where the things of God are concerned, the only balance you need is between the Word of God and the Holy Spirit. What part of "Love the Lord with all your heart, with all your soul, with all your strength" (Deuteronomy 6:5), implies that you should have some balance when it comes to the things of God? You cannot go too hard after God.

When we get to heaven, we will be amazed and awestruck at what we see when we see Father God. Father God won't be amazed when He sees us because we will still look the same to Him as we have our entire lives.

You are a new creation in Him. Embrace it, seek His face, spend time with Him, talk with Him, and most importantly, listen to Him.

HOW BIG IS YOUR "BUT"?

Throughout the Word of God, there have been ordinary men and women whom God has used to do great things. Each of them had a "but" that could have prevented them from accomplishing what God had for them. We do, too.

We have been placed here on this earth to love God and to accomplish His will. He could do it on His own, but He chose to partner with us to accomplish His will on the earth. Genesis 1:26 says we were made in Their image and after Their likeness, and have authority and dominion over all the earth. Adam's sin gave that away, but Jesus won it back through His death and resurrection.

John 14:12 (AMP) says, "I assure you, most solemnly I tell you, if anyone steadfastly believes in Me, he will himself be able to do the things that I do, and he will do even greater things than these, because I go to the Father."

We are sons and daughters of God, not going to be. We are sons and daughters the moment we accepted Christ as our Savior. It isn't something that we grow into or have to work up to. We simply are, once we have accepted Jesus as our Lord and Savior. As sons and daughters, we have authority. Remember what we just read in John 14:12 .

So why aren't we? Why aren't we taking authority and reigning here on the earth? Because our "buts" have gotten in the way. We all have them, some of us have more than others. Some of us have bigger ones than others. Have you ever said, "I'd do this for the Lord, but"? The "buts" have gotten the church where it is today. Many churches out there today are nothing more than big business, with no power, no anointing, just good motivational speaking (and some not even that).

We are not on this earth to just play with the world and try to get to the sweet by-and-by of heaven. We are here to have dominion, to subdue the earth, to occupy it, all while continuing to have a servant's heart.

As I said at the beginning of this chapter, many ordinary men and women throughout the Bible and throughout church history were used by God to do great things. I have heard this saying and it is so true, that God doesn't call the qualified, He qualifies the called.

- Abraham was old
- Noah didn't know want an ark was and had never seen rain
- Moses stuttered and was a murderer
- Gideon was hiding and was the least of his family from the least tribe
- Elijah was scared due to death threats against him
- Esther was just a teenager and risked death going before the king
- Jeremiah was too young
- Peter denied Jesus three times
- Paul killed believers
- Smith Wigglesworth couldn't read, had problems speaking and expressing himself
- My objection was insecurity, fear of failure, and no formal Bible training

What's your "but"? Too fat, too thin, too old, too young, your husband, your wife, your kids, your finances, never done anything like that, no Bible training, shyness, insecurity, fear?

The devil and your flesh will use your "but" to keep you from your identity as a son or daughter of God. Being kept from your identity will keep you from fulfilling God's plan and destiny for you.

Matthew 19:26 says "...With men this is impossible, but with God, ALL things are possible."

Philippians 4:13 says, "I can do ALL things through Christ who strengthens (empowers, enables) me." *(parentheses added).*

We were never meant to walk into our God-given destiny alone. God gave us the Holy Spirit to be with us every step of the way. It is time to draw the line in the sand and say, "Enough." It is time to stop letting your "but" keep you from walking in the authority and anointing that God has given you. Will you continue to allow your "but" to keep you from your destiny, or will you overcome it and walk in the fullness of that which God has for you?

TRUSTING GOD

Philippians 4:11-13 says, "Not that I speak in regard to need, for I have learned in whatever state I am to be content.

I know how to be abased, and I know how to abound. Everywhere and in all things I have learned both to be full and to be hungry, both to abound and to suffer need.

I can do all things through Christ, who strengthens me."

Being fully committed and submitted to God and His love puts you in a place of contentment, a place of trust in Him, because you know that you are His child and He isn't going to let you down. He isn't going to let you miss His will for your life as long as you are being obedient to Him, and His word is going to be fulfilled in your life.

Jeremiah 1:5 says that God knew us before we were formed and that He has sanctified us. That means that He has set us apart, consecrated us, and dedicated us. We have been specifically selected by our Father God. **Chosen.**

Are these just words to tickle our ears? Are these words to make us feel good about ourselves so that our self-esteem will be OK? No, these are words of life, words that should build our faith and trust in a Holy God: a God who wants to be our Father, a God who has sacrificed His Son so that a relationship may be opened between us and Him, a God who has freely given us His very Spirit, to be with us so that we will never be alone. John 15:16 tells us that we did not choose Him until He first chose us. We did not love Him until He first loved us, and Romans 5:8 tells us that He loved us and Christ died for us even when we were still sinners, serving ourselves and the enemy.

Webster's Dictionary defines the word "trust" as follows: "a firm belief or confidence in the honesty, integrity, reliability, justice of another person." Throughout the Bible, we see the character, integrity, and justice of God, so trusting God should be easy. "Faith" is defined by *Webster's Dictionary* as, "the unquestioning belief that does not require proof or evidence."

Hebrews 11:1 says, "Now faith is the substance of things hoped for, the evidence of things not seen."

Hebrews chapter 11, verse 1 sounds a lot like the definition in the dictionary. How can you have faith in something you don't trust? We put our faith and trust in things each and every day without having any sort of a real relationship or insight into it.

Every time you go to a light switch, you trust and have faith that it will turn on or off depending on what you are doing. Whenever you get in your car, you trust and have faith that it will start. When you fly in an airplane, you just board the plane and have faith and trust that the pilot knows what he's doing, and can both fly and land the plane safely. Have you ever boarded an airplane and asked the pilot if he knew what he was doing? Or if he knew how to get to your destination? No, you trust and have faith that the airlines would provide you with a pilot that would be able to get you to your destination safely. So why do you have such a hard time trusting and having faith in God?

Hebrews chapter 11 also tells us that it is impossible to please God without faith (see verse 6). Proverbs chapter 3 tells us to trust God with all our heart. Romans chapter 12 says that we have each been given a measure of faith. I don't believe we can have faith without trust, as the two go hand in hand. Think about any relationship that you have. For example, those of you who are married, think about the relationship with your spouse. You trust that person to remain faithful to you. You have faith that they will forsake all others. If there is infidelity in that relationship, trust is broken. When trust is broken, faith is also broken. People have the capacity to be untrustworthy; God does not. His Word says that He will always be with us and never forsake us (Hebrews 13:5). His Word says that His thoughts toward us are thoughts of peace to give us a future and a hope; when we call on Him He will listen and when we seek Him with all our heart we will find Him (Jeremiah 29:11-13). Does that sound like a Father God who cannot be trusted? He doesn't have to allow us to be a part of His plans here on the earth, but He has chosen us to be part of the plan.

Some may say that God has let them down because He didn't answer their prayer the way they thought He should. To those people, I would say that sometimes God's answer to people is "No." Sometimes, God's answer to our prayer is what we need, not what we want. That doesn't mean that He has forsaken you or that He doesn't love you.

Isaiah 55:8-9 says, "'For My thoughts are not your thoughts, nor are your ways My ways,' says the Lord.

'For as the heavens are higher than the earth, so are My ways higher than your ways, and My thoughts higher than your thoughts.'"

It's time that we stop trying to make God fit into our plans. We should be fitting into His plans. When this occurs, there won't be an opportunity for God to let us down because we are following His plan, and His plan for our lives will be fulfilled. Believing that God's thoughts and ways are higher than ours, coupled with the truth that God sees and knows ALL, should bring us to a place of trust. He sees the whole picture; we are only seeing the part that God reveals to us.

Romans 8:15 says that we have received the Spirit of adoption, praise God. We have been adopted, and therefore are partakers of the covenant relationship that God has between Himself and the Israelites as well as the new covenant. We have been engrafted into the family, partakers of the inheritance.

All too often, when we talk about God as Father, people get defensive and sometimes skeptical because they are attributing the character of their earthly fathers to their heavenly Father. Unfortunately, in the world today, there are too many absentee fathers, whether by actual abandonment of their children, or by virtual abandonment being workaholics, or satisfying their own selfish desires and pursuits. Some have fathers who are in the home, but are abusive or simply decide not to have a relationship with their children. The experience with our earthly fathers definitely impacts our relationship with Father God, and therefore our ability to accept the truth that we are sons and daughter of the Most High God. If we had any sort of dysfunctional relationship with our earthly fathers, many times, that dysfunction is projected onto our heavenly Father. Attributing the traits we experienced in our earthly fathers to our heavenly Father has the potential to cause issues with trusting in and having faith in God. It is essential that our experiences with our earthly fathers be dealt with and overcome so that we can receive the love of our heavenly Father. Our earthly fathers loved in the manner in which they knew, and in some cases, they parented out of their own hurt. Our Father God loves us with an unconditional love that knows no bounds, and has no limit. According to Romans chapter 8, verses 38-39, nothing can separate us from the love of God in Jesus, NOTHING and NO ONE.

Setting aside all that we have experienced so that we can receive the love that God has for us is a decision. Trust is a decision. Having faith is a decision. Will we believe what the Word of God says about who we are and what we were put on this earth to do? Will we believe and receive the promises that God has for us? Will we accept it as truth? If we do, then we will be able to overcome our past experiences and step into a realm where we are led by the Spirit of God and therefore are the sons of God (Romans 8:14).

INTIMACY & SONSHIP

Webster's Dictionary defines intimacy as "close familiarity, friendship, closeness." Intimacy implies a certain vulnerability because without opening yourself to another, you cannot achieve intimacy. Intimacy (INTO ME SEE) is a scary proposition to some people, because they believe that it will put them in a position to be hurt by others. While that is true to an extent, it also puts them in a position to be loved by others.

Looking back to the discussion of walls in our life, we can see how those walls prevent intimacy, both with those around us and with the Lord. It is essential to our place as sons of God to open ourselves up to the Spirit of God. God is omniscient. He knows everything, so when we hide from God, it's not like He doesn't know.

In the Garden of Eden, after Adam and Eve ate the fruit of the tree of the knowledge of good and evil, God came and asked Adam "Where are you?" It wasn't because God didn't know where they were. God didn't lose them. It was because Adam had removed himself from his position as a son.

In 1 Kings chapter 19, Elijah was hiding in a cave after fleeing from Jezebel's death threats. God came and asked him "What are you doing here, Elijah?" It was not because God didn't know why he was there or what had happened. He was asking Elijah, because Elijah had forgotten who he was in the Lord. He had momentarily forgotten that he was God's prophet. He had stepped out of his position and calling because of the words of Jezebel, his own imagination, and self-pity.

When we forget who we are, when we step out of our position as sons of God, the same thing will happen to us. The God-intended promises don't have the same hold or impact on our lives as they once did. We step out of intimacy with the Lord and begin to walk according to our flesh.

God wants us to stay in that intimate relationship with Him, walking in the Spirit, being led by the Spirit. That intimacy with the Father will allow us to hear the still, small voice when the Father speaks, that still, small voice that gives direction, encouragement, and love. When we walk in that place of intimacy with the Father, we become as Jesus was, His beloved son. Unless we are willing to be His beloved, we cannot become like Jesus.

John 15:4-5 says, "Abide in Me, and I in you. As the branch cannot bear fruit of itself, unless it abides in the vine, neither can you, unless you abide in Me.

I am the vine, you are the branches. He who abides in Me, and I in him, bears much fruit; for without Me you can do nothing."

The word "abide" in this passage of scripture means "to dwell permanently." Jesus said that if we dwell permanently in Him, and He dwells permanently in us, that we would bear much fruit. We can do nothing outside of Him. We cannot be sons outside of Him. We cannot love outside of Him.

How do we dwell permanently with Him? Make spending time with God your priority, not something you do if you have time. You may say, "I'm so busy that I can't afford to take time out for God." I would reply that you cannot afford to not spend time with God. Seek Him first, and He will redeem your time.

Intimacy with the Lord is not about seeking His hand or His provision. It is about seeking His face and a relationship with Him, seeking the Creator, rather than the creation. The time has come for us to seek a deeper relationship with God rather than more information about God. It is time to have an experience with God rather than more knowledge about Him. Information about God won't bring intimacy, but intimacy will bring information as God reveals Himself to us in the secret place with Him.

Romans 8:15 says, "For you did not receive the spirit of bondage again to fear, but you received the Spirit of adoption by whom we cry out Abba, Father (Daddy, Daddy)." *(parentheses added).*

In an earlier chapter, I spoke about the walls that we put up to protect ourselves. Those walls help us to numb the pain that was brought about by our experiences in life. That numbness means that you FEEL NOTHING. Unfortunately, when you are numb to the pain, you are numb to the love as well.

Religion shows you only how to numb the pain, ignore it or how to live with it. Religion does not deal with the symptoms or the cause of the pain, it only helps you to anesthetize it.

Intimacy with Father (Daddy) God is the cure for the numbness. Intimacy with the Lord removes the need to be anesthetized and forces you to deal with the cause of the pain with Him. This allows the Father to heal you once and for all.

However, many people have an issue with intimacy, because intimacy causes us to be naked, showing all of our stuff, and nakedness makes us uncomfortable. God is not interested in our comfort– He is interested in our healing. He is interested in our joy, and He is interested in our wholeness. Intimacy with Daddy God begins to strip away our walls and defenses before Him. Nobody likes to be naked, as it's so uncomfortable. The thing is, Daddy God already knows about all our stuff – He knew about our stuff before we did. Intimacy with Daddy God helps us to be open and honest with ourselves. Intimacy is also something that many people are uncomfortable with because they might have to take responsibility for themselves and the pain and disappointment they feel. Intimacy with Daddy God will bring us to a place of fulfillment and contentment that no amount of success and achievement ever will. When we reach that place of intimacy with Daddy God, our personal will and dreams will no longer drive us. We will be so in love with Him, and He with us, that we will be willing to put His will, His plans for us and His dreams for us before everything else.

Song of Solomon provides us with a picture of what that might look like.

Song of Solomon 3:1-4a, "By night on my bed I sought the one I love; I sought him, but I did not find him.

'I will rise now,' I said, 'And go about the city; in the streets and in the squares I will seek the one I love.'

I sought him but I did not find him.

The watchmen who go about the city found me; I said, 'Have you seen the one I love?'

Scarcely had I passed by them, when I found the one I love. I held him and would not let him go."

Do you have that kind of hunger for a relationship with Daddy God? Will you search for Him until you find Him? And when you find Him, will you never let Him go? Intimacy requires us to be open, honest, committed, and consistent.

The book *Spiritual Slavery to Spiritual Sonship* by Jack Frost (p. 12) provides the best definition of sonship that I have ever read:

"Sonship is a heart that feels at rest and secure in God's love; it believes it belongs, it is free from shame and self-condemnation, it walks in honor toward all people, and it is willing to humble itself before man and God. It is subject to God's mission to experience His love and to give it away."

Sons are meant to have a relationship with their fathers. Not just as an acquaintance, but an intimate relationship, where thoughts and dreams are shared. That is the kind of relationship that God wants us to have with Him, where we spend time alone with Him, getting to know Him and letting Him get to know us. As I have mentioned previously, God knows everything about us, but part of building our relationship with Him is for us to open ourselves up to Him. It helps build faith and trust on our part.

Sonship is that position I have been talking about throughout this book. Sonship is that place of love, warmth, security, a sense of belonging, home. Your true identity is to walk as a son. The mission that is mentioned in the quote from *Spiritual Slavery to Spiritual Sonship* is the Great Commandment that Jesus speaks of in Matthew 22:37-40 after one of the Pharisees asks Him the question, "Which is the great commandment in the law?"

Matthew 22:37-40 "Jesus said to him, 'You shall love the Lord your God with all your heart, with all your soul, and with all your mind.

This is the first and great commandment.

And the second is like it: You shall love your neighbor as yourself.

On these two commandments hang all the Law and the Prophets.'"

The mission, should you decide to accept it (with no apology to the Mission Impossible franchise), is to love God with all your heart, all your soul, and all your mind and to love your neighbor as yourself. Any other mission than that mission is ultimately the devil's mission. Intimacy with the Father breeds sons and daughters of God. Intimacy with the Father comes first. Everything in ministry is driven from that loving relationship with the Father. Intimacy before fruitfulness.

There are some believers who would say that the Great Commission is more important than the Great Commandment. If we put the Great Commission before love, then our motivation is wrong. It is out of love that we are to minister, or else we run the danger of doing things with a "notch in your belt" mentality, counting how many people we can get saved. The Bible says to go and make disciples of all nations, not just get people saved. Discipleship requires an investment in someone, a relationship with someone, not just a drive by. That investment, that relationship, is rooted in love, God's love being poured out.

CONCLUSION

Each of us has a race to run with God. That race is to love God, be loved by God, and pour His love onto others. However, each of our races will take a different course so that we can reach different people, based upon God's plans and purposes for our life.

Romans 8:15-16 (The Message) "This resurrection life you received from God is not a timid, grave-tending life. It's adventurously expectant, greeting God with a childlike 'What's next, Papa?' God's Spirit touches our spirits and confirms who we really are."

"Not a timid, grave-tending life" -- Wow, that puts it in perspective. This race we are to run should be run with expectancy and eagerness to see what God has next for us. We are supposed to be going from glory to glory, His Spirit confirming with our spirit who we are and what our true identity is as sons of the Most High God.

So I say to you today, choose to walk in the way that you were meant to walk. Choose to allow God to take down your walls, because when the walls come down, bridges are built. Choose to allow God to heal all your hurts, to set you free from your bondage, to make you whole and to provide you with His protection under the shadow of the Almighty.

Choose the identity that your Father God has for you as a son of God and a co-heir with Jesus. Choose to live a life as a partner of God, not a servant or a hireling. Choose to walk in an intimate relationship with Daddy God. Choose to love Him and be loved by Him.

For those of you who have read this book and don't know Jesus as your Lord and Savior, please take the opportunity now to believe in your heart and confess with your mouth that Jesus is Lord. He loves you and wants nothing more than for you to be healed, delivered and set free.

Please pray this prayer:

Father I ask for you to forgive my sin, I believe that Jesus died for me and that He rose again from the dead. Jesus, please be my Lord and Savior.

If you prayed that prayer, let me be the first to welcome you as a brother or sister. Now begin your adventure with Father God by spending time getting to know Him, through the Word of God (Bible), attending a Bible-believing church, and spending time in prayer talking and listening to Him. God Bless.

APPENDIX A
Suggested Reading

Spiritual Slavery to Spiritual Sonship, Jack Frost

Experiencing Father's Embrace, Jack Frost

Spiritual Authority, Watchman Nee

www.ingramcontent.com/pod-product-compliance
Lightning Source LLC
Chambersburg PA
CBHW071253070526
44583CB00017B/2455